AF228355

FORMULA ONE RACE CARS

A First Look

PERCY LEED

GRL Consultant, Diane Craig, Certified Literacy Specialist

Lerner Publications ◆ Minneapolis

Educator Toolbox

Reading books is a great way for kids to express what they're interested in. Before reading this title, ask the reader these questions:

What do you think this book is about? Look at the cover for clues.

What do you already know about Formula One race cars?

What do you want to learn about Formula One race cars?

Let's Read Together

Encourage the reader to use the pictures to understand the text.

Point out when the reader successfully sounds out a word.

Praise the reader for recognizing sight words such as *is* and *the*.

TABLE OF CONTENTS

Formula One Race Cars

A Formula One car is a kind of race car.

MANSELL
MOTORSPORT
JUDD
Power
DD&P
Reklame
STERN
J. Alesi
B.R.M
··Chronographes··
S-P-S
Group
Ford
EA AUTO
JUDD
Power
Martijn van Kalmthout

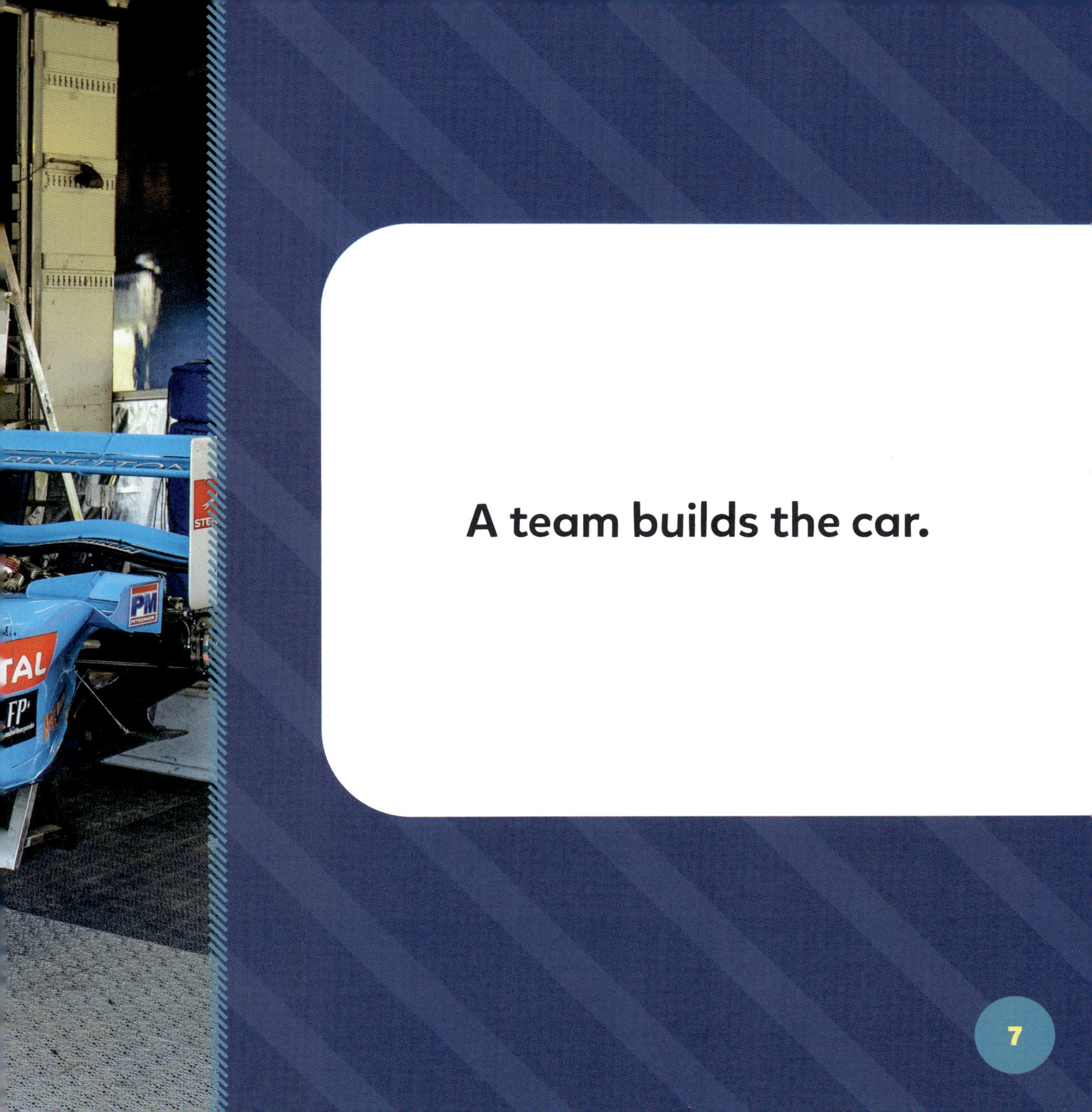

A team builds the car.

The car is not heavy.

It is built to be fast.

The engine sits in back.
It makes the car go.

Ferrari
engine

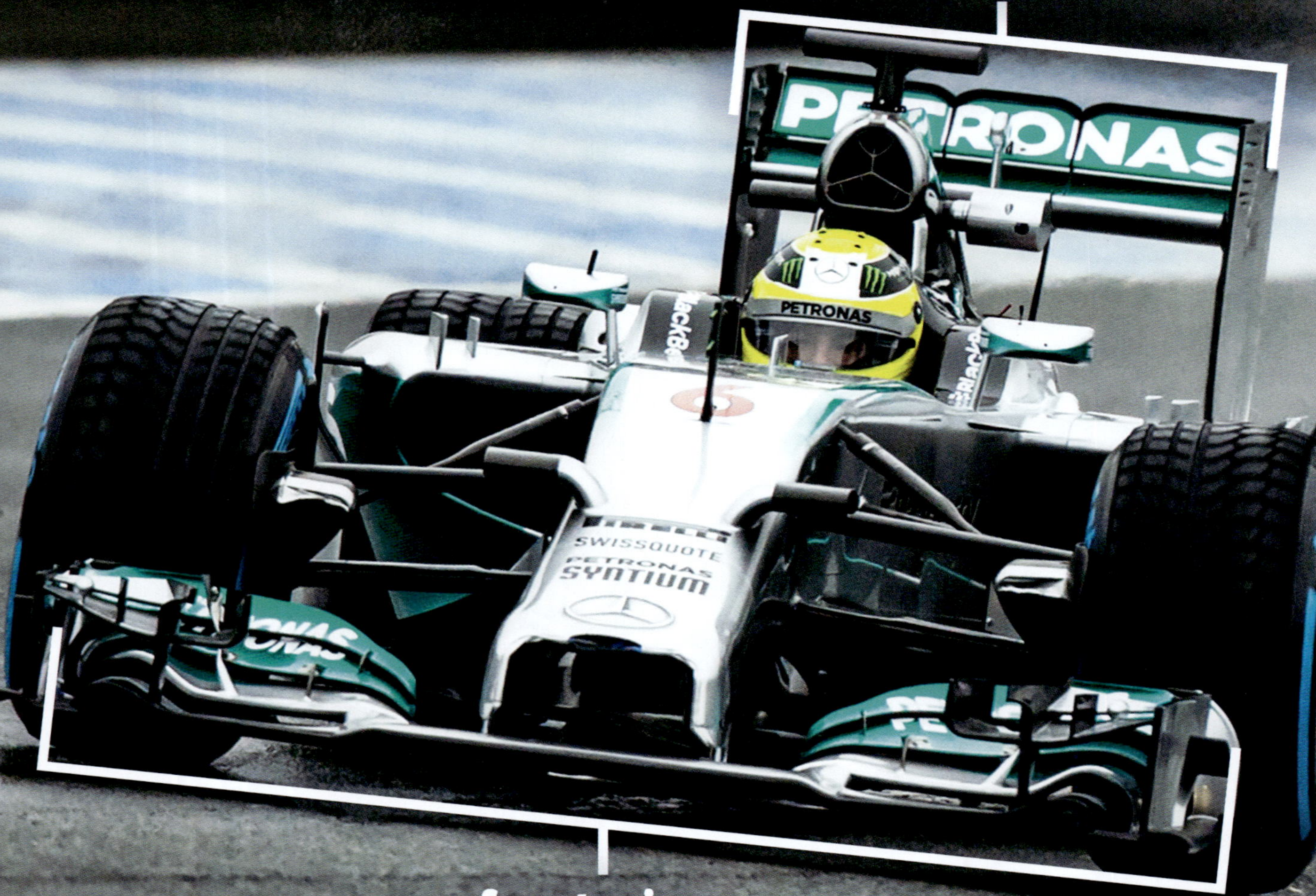

back wing
PETRONAS
PETRONAS
front wing

Air pushes down
on the wings.
This keeps the car
from tipping over.

The driver wears
a helmet.
He wears a seatbelt.
They keep him safe.

When do you
wear a helmet?

The cars speed around
the track.

The tires are often smooth.

17

The car makes
a pit stop.
It gets new tires.

19

Zoom! The driver wins the race!

You Connect!

Have you ever seen
a Formula One race?

Would you want to drive
a Formula One race car?

How can you learn more about
Formula One race cars?

STEM Snapshot

Encourage students to think and ask questions like scientists. Ask the reader:

What is something you learned about Formula One race cars?

What is something you noticed about Formula One race car parts?

What is something you still want to learn about Formula One race cars?

Photo Glossary

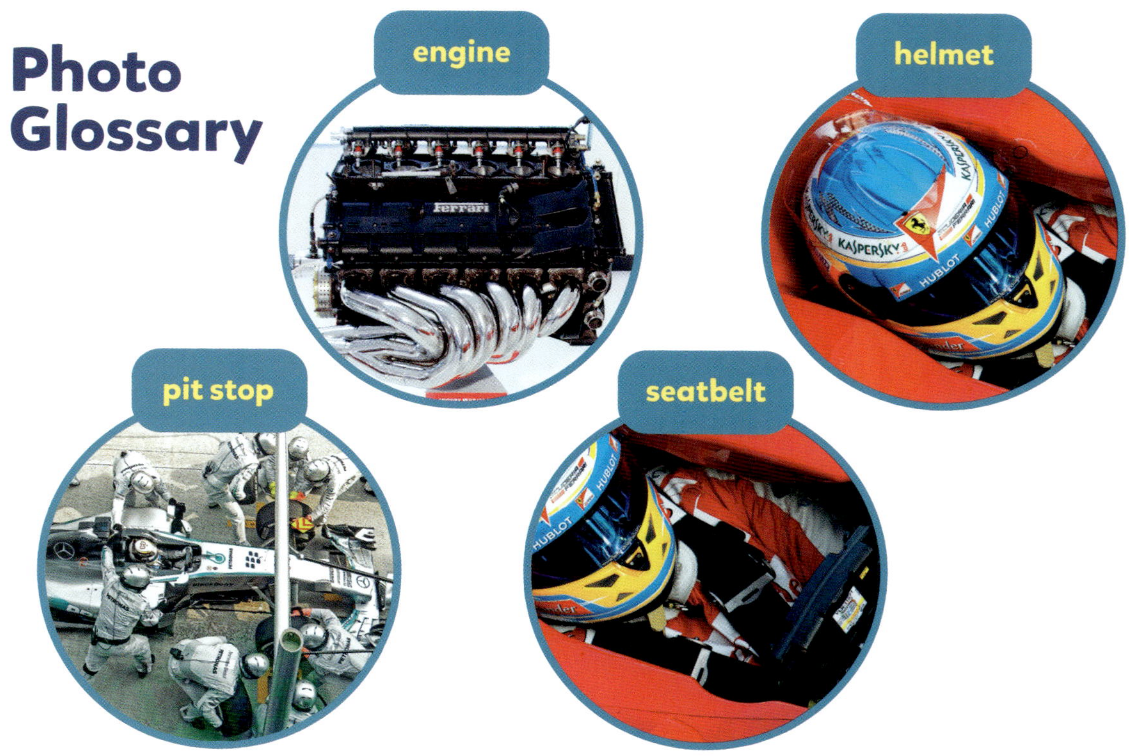

Learn More

Gish, Ashley. *Formula One Cars*. Mankato, MN: Creative Education, 2021.

Lewis, Katherine. *We Love Race Cars*. Minneapolis: Lerner Publications, 2021.

Storm, Marysa. *Formula 1 Cars*. Mankato, MN: Black Rabbit Books, 2020.

Index

Photo Acknowledgments

The images in this book are used with the permission of: © Ev. Safronov/Shutterstock Images, pp. 4–5; © Sjo/iStockphoto, pp. 6–7; © motorsports Photographer/Shutterstock Images, p. 8; © Michael Cola/Shutterstock Images, pp. 9, 16; © Natursports/Shutterstock Images, pp. 10–11, 17; © Zahorui Ivan/Shutterstock Images, pp. 11, 23 (engine); © MrSegui/Shutterstock Images, pp. 12–13; © ZRyzner/Shutterstock Images, pp. 14–15, 23 (helmet, seat belt); © Shahjehan/Shutterstock Images, pp. 18–19, 23 (pit stop); © ARprofessionals.com.my/Shutterstock Images, p. 20.

Cover Photograph: © Hafiz Johari/Shutterstock Images

Design Elements: © Mighty Media, Inc.

Lerner Publications Company
An imprint of Lerner Publishing Group, Inc.
241 First Avenue North
Minneapolis, MN 55401 USA

For reading levels and more information, look up this title at www.lernerbooks.com.

Main body text set in Mikado a Medium.
Typeface provided by Hannes von Doehren.

Library of Congress Cataloging-in-Publication Data

Names: Leed, Percy, 1968–author.
Title: Formula One race cars : a first look / Percy Leed.
Description: Minneapolis : Lerner Publications, [2024] | Series: Read about vehicles (Read for a better world) | Includes bibliographical references and index. | Audience: Ages 5–8 | Audience: Grades K–1 | Summary: "Formula One race cars are built to be fast and small, zooming around the track at high speeds. Thrilling photographs and easy text help readers understand how these race cars are different from the rest"—Provided by publisher.
Identifiers: LCCN 2022034682 (print) | LCCN 2022034683 (ebook) | ISBN 9781728491431 (library binding) | ISBN 9798765603628 (paperback) | ISBN 9781728499826 (ebook)
Subjects: LCSH: Formula One automobiles—Juvenile literature. | Automobile racing—Juvenile literature.
Classification: LCC TL236.265 .L44 2023 (print) | LCC TL236.265 (ebook) | DDC 629.228/5—dc23/eng/20221003

LC record available at https://lccn.loc.gov/2022034682
LC ebook record available at https://lccn.loc.gov/2022034683

Manufactured in the United States of America
2-1010569-51092-1/19/2024